CONCEALED

Finding Hope...While Hiding Pain

Sophia J. Brooks

CONCEALED
Finding Hope...While Hiding Pain

ISBN-13: 978-0692153437

Printed in the United States of America

First Printing, 2018

Front Cover Photography: Glesk Photos
Back Cover Photography: Erias Blackwell
Makeup: Julea Beauty Bar

The identities of certain people mentioned in this book have been left out or altered to protect their privacy.

Table of Contents

Dedication

To my Uncle Benji and Auntie Chant for trusting me with their newborn baby at a time when no one trusted me at all.

To my aunt, Beverly Rebecca Brooks, who has gone home to be with the Lord. This one's for you! ⚱

Foreword

When you are young, things have a way of getting out of proportion and running away with you. You can feel yourself being swept along on the crest of a tsunami of feelings. This leads you to a disconnection with your feelings and the love and care of those who are nearest and dearest, leaving the sufferer feeling isolated with the notion that they are alone and must do "this" on their own.

This is just the predicament that the young Sophia Brooks found herself in. In her mind, she was alone, isolated, and scared, with a secret that she could not trust anyone with. She was convinced that the world as she knew it would come crashing down around her.

It is with this backdrop that we begin the journey, walking with the author in the most intimate of places and discovering her true thoughts and the experiences of her young life. Although surrounded by family who loved her and friends who would have done anything to support her, she embarked on the loneliest journey that it's possible to go on. It involved pain, deception, and intrigue.

In this book, she shares her heart and journey with the reader as this story of redemption unfolds. She seeks to speak to her generation and those coming behind her with the hope that they will never have to experience the heartbreak and tragedy that have been so real to her.

She shows beyond a shadow of a doubt that your experiences are never just for yourself; your life and story can become a map for others, allowing them to avoid the mistakes that you didn't.

— Bishop Melvin and Pastor Yvonne E. Brooks

Acknowledgments

To God be the glory, great things He has done.

To God, my Father, I stand in awe of your love toward me and your grace and mercy that have been the shield surrounding me from the very day I was born. For the very breath that I breathe, I thank you. Though from time to time I am tempted to fall back into my reckless ways, you remind me of the pain and suffering I put myself and others through, which causes me to look back and remember the cross—the sacrifice you made so that I can receive everlasting life.

To my parents, Beverly Clark and Neville Brooks. You believed in me. When my back was against the ropes and all that people saw was the hell on earth I had created, you saw your little girl, your baby doll. I am truly grateful for your consistency in my life and for not allowing me to destroy myself.

To my father's wife and my mother by marriage, many things you didn't have to do but you did. You sacrificed so much and for that, please know I am forever grateful. I am amazed at the cities, states, and countries I have been able to travel to under your international ministry to bring hope to others and share the gospel in song.

To my amazing uncle and auntie, who were my bishop and pastor for so many years. You allow me to be who I am, unapologetically. I have learned so much from being under your ministry. I believe being there prepared me for a lot of the challenges I have experienced in the ministry today. I am reminded of what you told me after being away from the ministry for a year and having to come back and face the church membership: "Sophia, your biggest revenge is to become a massive success and by the virtue of your success, you put your enemies to public shame and disgrace." It has stuck with me every time I have felt defeated.

I have three amazing godparents whom I chose. Yes, I did! I call them my fairy godmothers. Deacon Beatrice Muldrow, Mother Eleam, and Elder Dorothy Young. Ms. Bea, you have truly been my safe place. You have guided me spiritually in this world called "church." So many things I never understood and you always directed me back to God. "Let it go, Sophia," is what you have told me and trust me, those words have saved my life. Thank you, Mother E, for your encouragement and your prayers. I am so glad God keeps showing Himself strong through your health and that you remain strong, steadfast, and unmovable. You are such an inspiration. And to Elder Dot, without whose help this project would have taken longer to complete. I love you and thank you.

Special thanks to my Uncles Delroy, Philip, and Junior Vassell, who assisted my father in redecorating the accommodation I was living in.

A special thank you to the Muir family...especially Ms. Joanne, for being a great support.

To my social worker Deborah Williams Ruth and also my counselor who met with me every week....thank you.

And to Mrs. S...thank you for still loving me!

To the rest of my family, from aunts and uncles, cousins, and especially my grandparents, I want to thank you all for sticking by me and for supporting me through the good, the bad, and the ugly. Even though the tough love and the absence of some of you in my life due to the events that occurred deeply pained me, I still say thank you. I wouldn't be the woman I am today had things turned out differently. I still remember running to my grandparents after a disagreement I had with one of my aunts. I ran up the stairs to my grandfather's room and threw open the door, and just cried my eyes out to him. He just let me pour out my heart. I had been avoiding him for days because I was so afraid of what he would say. I will never forget that moment! Words cannot express how thankful I am to you all and my prayer is that I continue to make you all proud of my accomplishments and future endeavors. Together we are a powerful force in the Kingdom of God. United we stand, divided we fall!

To my aunts, who nursed me back to health, who let me sleep in their bed, and listened to me cry myself to sleep at night; who prayed and stayed up with me and listened to me rant and rave about the things I was mad or sad about, and who forced me to eat when I didn't want to. I will never forget it. I really do have the best aunties in the world. I love you and thank you.

To Reverend Arlicia Albert of Beaumont, Texas, for your *Resuscitate Your Life Code Blue* workbook, which helped me regain the energy and passion I needed to finish this book.

To Dreams Academy of Akron, Ohio, for making one of my dreams come true.

I would like to thank my sister and friend, Miracle Reed, who helped me complete and finalize my book. You are a treasure and I am blessed to know you.

And to my precious little big baby boy. Mommy will see you in the sky one day. I will see you in the sky...

1

The Wages of Sin is Death

Every time we sin something dies,

whether we see it now or not...

The wages of sin is death.

I was going about my daily routine. I was living with a church sister in the UK who was a longtime family friend. It was a summer night and I was on my way home from church, walking and talking on the phone like it was a normal day. A short time later, I was sitting in the back of a police car in handcuffs. My life was no longer my own. I was now in the hands of the judicial system. I stared longingly at my house as we drove away, blue lights flashing on the homes that lined my quiet street. I rested my head against the seat and closed my eyes. How had I gotten here?

Has there ever been a time in your life when you have sinned against God or hurt your family and friends? God has provided us with family, friends, and others whose sole purpose is to help us in our time of need.

There are two scriptures I would like to share with you.

Ephesians 6:2: *Honor thy father and mother; which is the first commandment with promise.*

Exodus 20:12: *Honor thy father and thy mother: that thy days may be long upon the land which the Lord thy God gives thee.* (KJV)

While growing up, especially during my teenage years, I did not respect my parents nor did I honor them. I believed they had failed me. But one thing I do know, now that I have a better understanding of the scriptures, is that I do not want to die before my time. I do not want people to see "gone too soon" on my grave. I want to leave this earth knowing that I have fulfilled my purpose and I have successfully finished my course. If honoring my parents is one of the requirements to make it to Heaven to experience a long life with my Heavenly Father, then so be it.

My parents tried to be there for me during this time but I didn't want to acknowledge it. I believed my father had abandoned me and my mother had given up on me. I believed I was independent and on my own. Covering my lies became the norm and I had moved from unbearable pain into a state of numbness. My deepest, darkest secret was no longer mine. It was now public. But even then I saw God's hand in every area. The story of what I had done reached the local newspaper but no names were mentioned. It could have reached the TV but members of the church I attended kept my trust. For that, I am grateful.

As you read my story, you will note that I frequently revisit this time in my life. I pray that you too will look at your own life and reflect on the deepest, darkest secret you have. I hope you will ask God to deliver you and set you free from the bondage that haunts you and tells you that you will never get past this, that you will never receive complete healing.

Confide in a mentor, your pastor, or a life coach. Invite them on this journey with you. If you're ready for change, all you have to do is ask God to deliver you and watch Him do the rest!

This is my life.

This is my story.

2

Who Am I?

My name is Sophia Brooks. I was born in 1986 to Neville and Beverly and grew up in Wolverhampton, England along with my older sister. My father is a pastor and my mother was a worship leader. I grew up in an Apostolic Pentecostal church with those good old hymns I used to sing along to but never knew the correct words—songs like "Blessed Insurance," "Jesus is Mine," and "Lord Beware Me, To Be A Sanctuary." Funny but true. Seeing and hearing my mother singing so beautifully cultivated my own love for singing.

Growing up, I was definitely a girly girl and I loved getting ready for church, wearing frilly socks and dresses, glossy shoes, and having my hair washed and braided with bobbles that matched my outfits. Those were the days! My mother is such a lady and she made sure her girls looked coordinated, fresh, and clean. I loved being a pastor's child then (not so much now, as an adult).

I grew up in a traditional home, watched little TV unless it was educational or the news, and I never wore trousers, jewelry, or makeup. The makeup and jewelry did not bother me as a child, but the trousers? That really annoyed me as a young girl growing up. Having to go on field trips wearing denim skirts ALL the time....let me tell you, I thank God for the day that He changed my father's mind.

I was eight or nine years old when my father surprised me and my sister and bought us some Adidas sweatpants—or as the English say, tracksuit bottoms. I was in utter shock. I couldn't believe it! I said, "What are these?" I obviously knew what they were, I just always had to say something. My father said, "Oh, you don't want them?" I laughed and said, "No, Dad, it's fine."

Another time we went on a family outing and pulled up to Showcase Cinemas. I said to my father, "Dad, what are we doing here? We are not allowed to come here." So my dad answered, "Do you want to leave and go home?" I screamed, "Nooo!"

The first movie my sister and I watched at the movie theater was *Space Jam* with Michael Jordan. I was ten years old. I still think it's the best movie ever made.

The reason my father had a lot of strong, traditional views when I was a child is because of the way he was raised. He was a preacher's kid. My father's father, my grandfather, is a bishop who is now in his mid-80s and is still preaching the gospel (praise the Lord). My father is the second of ten children and seven of his siblings are in the ministry. When my father started his own ministry, independent of my grandfather, it devastated the whole family. I remember one of my aunts saying it was like there was a black cloud over our grandparents' home. Because of this, my sister and I were not allowed to visit for a period of time.

To grow up as a pastor's kid, for me, wasn't hard until my parents divorced in 1995. It is also difficult now, as an adult, watching people disrespect my parents as they pastor now.

I became very bitter and angry. My sister and I witnessed many arguments between our parents. I didn't trust my mother and I didn't trust my father. I believe at that time I had more anger toward my mother because I felt she held the keys to my future and whether I would be living in a broken home or a family home. A marriage is supposed to be forever, for life! You are supposed to love your wife and you are supposed to love your husband. I didn't understand why divorce had to happen to my family but it did. That's life!

When life comes at you fast and furious, it is not the time for you to move *away* from God, it's time for you to draw *nigh* to Him. It's easy for me to say this now, as an adult, but as a child, I was not thinking that way. I wanted my family to stay together and I felt that this God that I had been brought up to serve was allowing this to happen.

I remember being in the living room when my father was trying to explain to his two daughters, with tears in his eyes, how sorry he was for what was happening in our lives. This was the first time I saw my father cry and it broke my heart. For a child, your father is your hero. Like my dad says, the father is the one who gives you identity; he tells you who you are. (A few scriptures regarding how God gives identity can be found in John 1:12 and John 15:15.)

One minute, my father was there, the next he was no longer present in the home. He was only a ten-minute car ride away but to me, that wasn't great. I didn't realize that soon he would be miles and miles away. I was only ten. My father needed to just come home and stop this foolishness.

Our days with our dad were Wednesday nights and Saturdays and I cherished those moments. McDonald's, KFC, Pizza Hut, anything we asked for, he gave us. I absolutely loved my time with Dad. Finally, he was taking time for us. It wasn't always about church, a church meeting, or church people. It was just about *us*, me and my sister. And that's all we really wanted. I would think from time to time, *Why don't these people call Jesus? My dad can't save them.*

As children, teenagers, and even young adults, we tend to go to our parents for everything. There is absolutely nothing wrong with this and don't let anyone tell you otherwise. Your parents are definitely a LIFE SOURCE. It is a fact. Whether you had a deadbeat dad, an absentee mother, or parents who were physically in the home but not there emotionally for you, they are still your parents.

However, we always need to remember that God is our Father. He wants us to rely on Him, trust Him, cry to Him, praise Him, and worship Him. We are created to worship Him. He is our source.

Psalms 46:1 tells us: *God is our refuge and strength, our very present help in trouble.*

I thought there was something wrong with me when my parents divorced. One thing I have learned when it comes to other people's problems is...do not take them on.

David tells us in Psalms 139:14: *I am fearfully and wonderfully made, marvelous are thy works.*

God made you beautiful. Be happy with you. God cannot lie and He makes no mistakes! Nobody can be you except you, so be the best you that you can be. God is yearning for us to give everything over to Him. He wants to fix our problems. He wants to rescue us in times of trouble and despair but we are so reliant on ourselves that we often fail. The Psalms say trust in the Lord with all your heart, and lean not to your own understanding but in all your ways, acknowledge Him and He will direct your path.

I saw and heard a lot of things a child should not hear, not only from my parents but from others. What do we do with the things we see that are negative? Well, I'll speak for myself. I buried them, physically and spiritually. We are all made differently. For my sister, the divorce affected her differently. If there is a parent reading this and you are going through a divorce or separation, death or sickness, and you have more than one child, remember that everyone reacts differently. Never compare your children. This is something I detest, especially with family. No one is the same and no child will act the same way.

A few years ago, my father had a very serious scare involving cancer. It rocked our entire household. He had to undergo a surgery that normally takes ten hours; five hours to get to the tumor and another five hours to repair and put everything back together. I was determined to be there for him and his spouse however I could. I didn't understand why my sister couldn't be there and my father had to tell me that not everyone handles things the same way. Even in that, I learned a very valuable lesson. He said she was there the best way she knew how and he was fine with it.

I never thought about what my mother or father were going through. Divorce is just like death—the death of a family, death of a marriage, and the death of two souls intertwined together. The devil hates marriage because it is the image of God (I got that from my father).

Marriage was God's idea. Malachi 2:15 says that God makes it clear that it was He who "made them one." A covenant is an unbreakable commitment to one another. God wants us to know how very serious it is to make that vow. When a husband or wife choose to break such a sacred covenant, it tells God that His idea did not work.

God calls the church the "Bride of Christ" in 2 Corinthians 11:2 and He is coming back for us. God would never break his promise to us because He cannot lie and His word does not return void.

Numbers 23:19 says: *God is not a man, that He should lie, neither the son of man that he should repent: hath he said, and shall he not do it? Or hath he spoken, and shall He not make it good?* (KJV)

I love the New International Version. It says: *God is not human, that he should lie, not a human being, that he should change his mind. Does he speak and then not act? Does he promise and not fulfill?*

It gives me great joy to know that He is coming back for me. The feeling of shame and rejection that comes with divorce is devastating. It was rough going to the church that both our parents helped build and seeing our mother's seat empty and our father preach while he was hurting inside. The enemy will do anything he can to destroy marriage! That's why I encourage husbands and wives to seek counsel if you are having problems in your relationship. Go up and not down. What I mean by that is, do not go to your peers, your sisters, or your brothers.

Go to highly skilled people who are trained to deal with relationships and marriage. Not everybody can handle your story.

I recently attended a seminar where the pastor at my church was given the subject "God Will Reconcile" to teach. She said something so profound regarding relationships in the church. She said, "Do not bleed all over the church."

Just think about that. It was so powerful to me. All I could think about was how many times we tend to trust our fellow brothers and sisters in Christ. We tell them that we are mad at the preacher, we talk about the pastor, the praise-and-worship leader, the deacon, and the elders, then we are surprised when it gets back to the people we were talking about. So when it comes to marriage, it's even worse.

God hates divorce.

Malachi 2:16 NIV says, *"For I hate divorce!" says the LORD, the God of Israel. "To divorce your wife is to overwhelm her with cruelty," says the LORD of Heaven's Armies. "So guard your heart; do not be unfaithful to your wife."*

In our case, it was my mother divorcing my father.

Matthew 18:16 says: *But if he will not hear thee, then take with thee one or two more, that in the mouth of two or three witnesses every word may be established.* (KJV).

I think it would have helped me to know that my parents did try to work it out and that both sides were heard.

I will say that my father became a better father after he separated from my mother. It is sad to say but that's how it worked out. He wanted to make it clear to us that he was not an absentee father. He was present and he would continue to be present in our lives. I guess you could say I received a little bit of comfort through those words but it didn't bring my parents back together.

On Sunday mornings, we would get ready for church and leave Mom behind. My mother not only divorced my father but she also left the church. I remember her very words: "The church is full of hypocrites." Although our relationship at the time wasn't great, that statement stayed with me for a very long time.

I have a picture on my Facebook page as my cover photo that reads: "Be polite to all but intimate with few." I think my mother confided in people that she trusted but sharing her frustrations with just one person in that church was one too many. They ran with whatever information they were given and instead of my mother's words being held in confidence, it turned into a virus that spread all over the church. Words that were never said were added and it all became a big mess. She trusted people who couldn't handle the information correctly.

Listen, not everyone can handle your business and not everyone can handle your story. I asked Jesus to never, ever allow me to be a pastor's wife. I pray He gives me the desire of my heart. It seems so difficult. You trust people you think will have your back but in return, they stab you—not in your back but right in your heart.

Pastors are human. Your leaders are human. At our church recently, parents have been talking about putting people who hold titles up on a pedestal. Soon they will fall or make a mistake. I learned this at a very early age, having parents in the ministry. We cannot put our expectations on people. They are HUMAN. I cannot stress it enough. God did not make us perfect. Only He is perfect in all His ways.

Well, divorce was an option for my family. One thing we cannot do is change the past. But we can always change our future.

3

In My Father's House Are Many Mansions

The Lord laid upon my father's heart a conference called "First Things First!" After the guest speaker for the conference canceled, my father called a friend in Ohio and asked if she knew an unmarried female speaker—preferably a divorced mother so she could relate to our single ladies. She said she knew three. So she suggested that they fast and pray for the next three days and she would give him the name he needed on the fourth day.

The name she gave him was Elder Connie Mock from Pittsburgh, Pennsylvania. When I first saw her I was amazed! She was such a LADY, so warm and beautiful, with a big heart. My sister and I instantly formed a bond with her. We had girl talk, we felt safe speaking to her about some of the things we were going through, and she also had children around the same age as us.

The Bible says in Proverbs 18:22, *Whosoever findeth a wife findeth a good thing, and obtaineth favor of the Lord.* (KJV)

Well, my daddy found a good thing and soon he and Connie were engaged. At the time, I knew this but when they decided that he would be moving to the U.S., my heart broke all over again. Was this really happening? My father would be 3,000 miles away! That meant I couldn't see him by car, only by plane. Like the famous Sweet Brown says, "Ain't nobody got time for that." I would probably go from seeing him twice a week to once or twice a year. At twelve years old, my world as I knew it was over. While for my father it was a good thing, I selfishly saw it as a bad thing. I did not see the pros, I saw the cons. I did not see the positives, I saw the negatives. I did not see the possibilities that lay before me. I just knew that my father was leaving. How could he leave us? How did he think this was the best thing to do?

I remember sitting in my room crying. I was devastated. My father would be leaving not just us but the church he and my mother had planted, and my sister and I would have to continue to see these people. Already feeling the way I did, I didn't want to be bothered with the members looking at me with pity and sympathy. After the divorce, at least half, if not more, of the leaders left

16

our church. I felt that my father was unhappy but he soldiered on and continued pastoring.

This move meant that my father wouldn't be polishing my shoes at night before school, he wouldn't be taking us out to dinner and to the movies anymore, he wouldn't be at any family functions, and he wouldn't be surprising us at school and picking us up. It would just be me and my sister. Christmas, holidays, and birthdays would never be the same. Depressing, right?

At some point in your life, you might feel rejected or that you are not good enough. This is when you push through your emotions and press into the Word to build your spirit. When I need more of God, I read Psalms and Proverbs. Psalms helps you express your emotions with praise and adoration to the Father. Proverbs advises you and it's a book of wisdom and understanding.

My father gave me and my sister the news in the car outside our house. I mean, he could have chosen a better location. (Men! Lol.) He shared a scripture with us: *In my Father's house are many mansions: if it were not so, I would have told you. I go to prepare a place for you* (John 14:2, KJV). Our father told us he was going to prepare a place for us. (Blank stare.) Man, I did not want to hear that! How long would that take? What about Mom here and our family here? I couldn't see the benefits. I *refused* to see the benefits. I mean, Pastor Connie was nice and all but I didn't *really* know her. She could have been an ax murderer, a wicked stepmother...you just don't know people these days.

I laugh now because that's exactly what I was thinking at the time. I thought my dad had lost his mind. I didn't say a word in the car, which is surprising, and it was probably surprising to my dad because I am the one who always speaks up and has to say something. After he finished going on and on, I jumped out of the car and slammed the door behind me, ran to my room, and sobbed like a baby. All of these thoughts began to run through my head. *Why does he have to leave? Why can't she come here? I wonder how Mom must feel? What is the rush? You don't even know this woman. It's not fair! How could he leave us?*

My father married within six months. My sister and I were a part of his big day and it meant so much to us, as not many of our family could make it to the States. My grandma (Dad's mom) and our oldest cousin came to support him in his union. I honestly did not know what to call his wife at the time. Were we supposed to call her Pastor, Sister, Stepmom? I had no clue so we asked Pops and he asked us to call her Pastor Connie or Sister Connie. We didn't know she didn't like it at the time. She treated us just like her own, never called us stepchildren, and always called us her daughters! If you hear her story, you will know exactly why she treated us this way.

Now, in normal circumstances a newly married couple has no kids, they are able to go on their honeymoon, enjoy each other for a couple of years, then start a family. Well, that's my opinion. I didn't understand then that "the parents" would never really live by themselves and this situation was new not just for us but also for them. I was surely just thinking about myself.

The wedding was absolutely beautiful. My sister and I were already accustomed to getting our hair done professionally but for this wedding, I was so happy with all the things we were able to do. Nails, toes, hair, and even a little bit of makeup. Not that we needed it but I was so excited. Looking back at the pictures, my hair looked like it was a wig. All my long hair never looked so good! I was amazed at the way Pastor Connie did things with such excellence. It was a beautiful day.

My father's wife never let a Christmas or birthday go by without gifts upon gifts, and on Valentine's Day, a day we never celebrated (we Christians really have to lighten up about things like this) we would receive cards from her and Dad and we knew it wasn't his idea. I knew that my dad was changing for the better.

My sister and I had always wanted another brother. Well, with this union we gained two big brothers and another sister! Be careful what you wish for!

Blended families are hard work. We collided before we blended. And what a challenge it was—and still can be. You're either going to make the most of the people you have gained or you're going to be an absolute nightmare. I chose to be a nightmare. I did get along with all of my siblings. Obviously, I was closer with the sister I had gained than the brothers but we really did go through a lot. Our older brother was not living in the family home but my other three siblings and I gave our parents more than enough to work with. I wasn't thinking that the family I had gained had really lost anything by gaining us, but they did. Although they still had their mother, she would now have to share her time, her money, and her home.

Every summer from the time my father got married, he and Pastor Connie made sure they sent for me and my sister. They always made sure we had clothes for school. Even when my father first moved to the U.S. and was unemployed for a period of time, we never went without. I am so glad those years are over and I know they are too.

Pastor Connie says she prays that one day I will have a child who is just like me. I rebuke that in the name of Jesus because I know that I was a TRIP.

4

Looking for Love in All the Wrong Places

Well, four years had passed and in that time my sister had gone to live with my father. Within that four-year period, we had stopped attending the church my father had once pastored. We didn't like it. We (including my mom) started to attend our uncle's church (my dad's older brother) in a city about a thirty-minute drive away. We loved it. The praise and worship were amazing and the Word was good. We felt God's love and His presence.

My mother later left the church but my sister and I continued to go using public transportation. Mom would drop us off at the metro or train station and we would either catch the bus from the station to church or our cousin would pick us up if we were early enough. We hated the commute but we loved going to that church.

Things were becoming difficult at home with my mom and my older sister so that's when my sister went to live with my father. Now it was just me and Mom living together. It was difficult but I was trying to make the most of it. We had days when money was tight but she always made sure we ate. I got myself a little part-time job delivering newspapers after school, which paid about ten to fifteen pounds a week. I HATED it. I think I was about thirteen or fourteen and felt like I needed my own money.

I became a member of my uncle's church, serving the Lord on Sunday and talking to my mom like she had no sense on Monday. I missed my sister so much. I know I had some anger and resentment toward her for leaving me. I was the baby and we were so close growing up. We did everything together! I honestly believed I was completely on my own.

I took on the mindset of *I can do it by myself, I don't need your help.* Dad left, my sister left, and I was left by myself. Either way, I felt I was always going to feel abandoned. There was a lot of negativity within the home, especially about my father and what he was not doing. My mother didn't share every detail about their marriage but some things children should not know, period. Bear in mind I was a teenager but still, parents, keep your children out of adult business.

My mother was angry, hurt, and bitter and I was

following right behind her. That's what divorce can do, but remember *you* have the power to change your mindset; *you* have the power to change your outlook. As a child, you don't think about your parents' feelings. As I got older, I realized my mother had experienced a loss too. It wasn't all about me. Her husband—the man she had given her life to—and then her firstborn child had literally packed up and moved not down the road but across the ocean. I know the amount of emotion she went through at that time had to be difficult. I don't really remember anybody being there for my mother except my auntie. None of the people in the church she had helped build and no pastor or pastor's wife she had built relationships with over the years were there for her.

Unfortunately, the body of Christ—not He Himself but His bride—can cause so much pain and that was not God's plan for his bride. Nobody really wants a divorce, although at the time it was the easy way out. I don't think my mother was prepared for the events that took place. Dad found someone else, he was in love with someone else, and his daughters would soon follow him.

While still living in England with my mother and being extremely active in the church, at the age of sixteen I became promiscuous and it nearly ruined a very close relationship I had with an awesome friend of mine. Our relationship has never been the same since. I didn't have multiple partners but that was the age I got myself involved in a situation I had no business being in. I still can't believe it to this day. Looking back now, at the age of thirty-one, I see how foolish and stupid I was. I just wanted to feel the love that I felt I was missing. Clearly, it was not *that* kind of love I needed.

God does not want this for you. Sex of any kind is supposed to be within a marriage between a man and a woman. Sex was made for marriage! Hebrews 13:4 says, *Marriage is honorable in all and the bed undefiled: but whore mongers and adulterers God will judge* (**KJV**). 1 Corinthians 6:9-10 says, *Or do you not know that the unrighteous will not inherit the kingdom of God? Do not be deceived; neither fornicators, nor idolaters, nor adulterers, nor effeminate, nor homosexuals, nor thieves, nor the covetous, nor drunkards, nor revilers, nor swindlers, will inherit the kingdom of God* (**KJV**).

My father always says men are visual; they go after what they see. At sixteen years of age, we are all physically developing or are already developed. My pastor has always said that a Christian woman should let the Holy Spirit be her guide and He will tell you whether something is too low or too tight. I love the fitted look so I have to be careful when choosing something to wear on a Sunday morning. Don't be too quick to show off all your goodies. Save all of that for your husband and let your husband be the one to uncover your beauty! You are a child of God, a princess, a queen, a prince, a king. Come on, men, you know when your trousers are too tight and your shirt is exposing all of your GREAT muscles.

Psalms 27 says, *Wait on the Lord and be of good courage, He will strengthen your heart, wait I say on the Lord'* (KJV).

I wish I had waited! And too many of us have that statement lingering in our heads. For all those who may have gone before God and done things your own way, He can restore you!

I remember sitting in one of my dad's classes at the church with the young people. It was called "Sex, Lies, and Videotape," a program to educate them about the dangers of getting into relationships before their time and what the Bible says about waiting. Something he said in that class has stuck with me to this very day. Back in his day, he explained, there were probably one or two sexually transmitted diseases and they could be treated with antibiotics. Today, there are many more and not all of them can be effectively treated. Do you know that I thank God even to this day for protecting me and shielding me from such diseases? Whew! Glory praise break right here.

2 Chronicles 7:14 says: *If my people, which are called by my name, shall humble themselves, and pray, and seek my face, and turn from their wicked ways; then will I hear from heaven, and will forgive their sin, and will heal their land.* (KJV)

I am a Christian. I am called by His name. God will still give you chance after chance to change, to make a 180-degree turn. He is a merciful and just God; He is mighty to save, mighty to deliver and set free. He is also a jealous God. Be careful not to put anything or anyone before Him. Today, I thank God for life. I thank God that He saved me.

If you are a promiscuous young woman or man, choose abstinence today! Go straight to your nearest clinic as soon as possible and get checked. The sooner you make that decision to go, the better. You don't know what God might be saving you from. Sometimes you don't even know you have caught something because you have no symptoms. Isn't that something?

Paul says in Romans, *I beseech you therefore, brethren, by the mercies of God, that ye present your bodies a living sacrifice, holy, acceptable unto God, which is your reasonable service.* (Romans 12:1 KJV)

We are to live holy. Our bodies are a work of art and we are made in the image of God. When you smoke, drink to get drunk, or have sex with anyone and everyone, you are destroying your body and it hurts God. I cannot raise my filthy hands on a Sunday morning if I was fornicating the night before. Yes, God is merciful but there are consequences to every action.

While having a discussion with my father, he shared that every time we sin, we put Jesus right back on that cross—the nails in His hands and His feet, the spear in His side, the whips on His back and the crown of thorns on His head.

He did it all for us. We crucify Him all over again

when we choose to sin. If we continue to sin, judgment will fall.

And judgment fell on me...

5

Moving Up Outta Here

A year before I graduated, I was turning sixteen. I
was so excited because the parents would be coming
over from the U.S. to celebrate with me. I spoke to my
sister regularly—well, as much as I could—and I asked
her if she was coming. I knew the answer but of course, I
had to ask. She couldn't come because of school, which
was disappointing, but I was just happy that the parents
would be there.

The day finally came, my parents were coming! I was
at school in the cafeteria with my girlfriends eating a
cheese-and-onion pasty, being all loud and boisterous as
usual, and my friend said to me, "Oh my gosh, isn't that
your sister?" I looked up and said, "Girl, no, please! I
told you she couldn't make it." And then I looked behind
me and saw my two sisters and brother walk into the

cafeteria. I screamed so loud! Such an amazing feeling! It was the best birthday I ever had. Everybody came and it was all for me. I thought, *Wow, all this for me?* I was sincerely overjoyed with excitement and that whole weekend was spent with them and my family in Birmingham.

I had never had a birthday party in all my sixteen years. Isn't that something? I look back now and I don't think I missed having parties because my family always made a big thing about birthdays and they still do. I guess my parents were just not too good at parties.

I successfully finished high school in July 2003, THANK YOU, LORD! I was planning to go to college but things at home became unbearable. My mother and I were always arguing and I knew she couldn't wait to see the back of me. Like I said before, I was a TRIP! But at some point, you have to take responsibility for your own actions. I can't blame my mother for everything. She did the best she could at the time. My uncle and aunt offered to take me in but my mother wanted me to go live with my father. I did not want to move at all. And here again, I felt rejected. Why was this happening? I did not want to leave my family and friends and I didn't want to move so far away. This was my father's life, not mine.

The decision was made and I moved to the U.S. that year in December. The airport scene was the worst. All my older cousins came to see me off and I just cried like a baby.

Coming to the States was definitely culture shock. Everything is so much bigger in America. And I would be going back to school! Even though I had just finished high school in England that summer, Americans don't finish school until they are eighteen (rolling my eyes). I absolutely hated the fact that I had to go back to school, especially in a foreign country.

I tried to keep quiet in school but as soon as I opened my mouth to speak there were twenty questions. Where are you from? Why did you move here? Are you really English? But you're black...are there black people in England?

I started the eleventh grade in January 2004 and helped out at the church where my parents pastored when I could so I could get some pocket money. At that time, the parents had one church in two locations.

It took over a year and a half for me to get my green card, so I was grateful for the hours Pastor Connie gave me at church. I worked alongside the church secretary at the time. We became very close and I learned a lot about administration. To this day, I call her my fairy godmother because, just like in Cinderella, she always calls or shows up in the nick of time.

It was so surreal. Many times I would sit and think, *Am I really living in America?* I had opportunities before me but could not see them. The open doors were right in front of me but I could not lift my feet to walk through them. The new family and new people God had put into

31

my life I somehow could not receive. The transition was hard and I chose to see every negative part of it.

I graduated high school in 2005 with a diploma with honors. I was now an American high-school graduate. That was a WOW moment for me. I was truly grateful and thankful that I would never have to go back to education unless I chose to do so. I decided to go to community college before transferring to a university. After all, I had received my green card by this time and I had a part-time job.

Things seemed to be coming together when looking at it from the outside but internally, I was a rotten apple. I always stayed in my room. My parents had to tell me to come out to join the family to watch a movie or go out. I honestly think I was secretly depressed. I didn't share anything with my parents. I kept to myself and that's how life was for me at that time.

I remember having an argument with my dad in the kitchen and I know I said something smart. He came right up to me, lifted me up by the tops of my dressing gown, and said, "While you're living in this house you will abide by my rules." Then he put me down and I stomped all the way to my room and slammed my door. He followed me up those stairs and I now have amnesia because I can't remember what came next. The cheek I had but I really did not care.

I am the type of person who is very adventurous and I like to try different things, especially when it comes to hair, so I asked Pastor Connie one day if I could cut my hair. It was breaking off anyway and I definitely wasn't going to ask Dad. But I wanted a change, she said yes, and I was elated. A couple of years earlier, I wanted to pierce my ears—I think I was thirteen. She said yes. This was big, especially coming from a family that was forbidden to do such things. My personal conviction is that as long as it isn't excessive, it's all good. I am still a child of the King, who loves Him. It's the heart that God is looking at.

My father had found his good thing, his wife. At the time, I was so selfish. I can honestly say I was happy for them but the happiness didn't last long. It would come and go. At the end of the day, I hadn't asked to be in America. I was told I had to be there.

I would lie, steal, and disrespect my parents until they couldn't take it anymore. They put me in counseling, which I was open to. It was something they called "Theo Therapy"—a biblically based form of counseling. I can say it helped as I was able to freely talk about my feelings to someone I knew would not judge me. But by then it was too late. I had been arrested, gone to court, and made the same mistake a second time and that was the final straw.

Pastor Connie said this to me and it has stuck with me ever since: "When your peace is disturbed within your home, something has to shift."

That something was me. Whether I wanted to or not,

I was going back to England.

But wasn't that what I wanted?

Generational Curses

It is very important for generational curses to be broken over your lifetime and over your children's children's lives. During a family Bible class with Pastor Connie a couple of months ago, she shared with us a scripture that says, *Only take heed to thyself, and keep thy soul diligently, lest thou forget the things which thine eyes have seen, and lest they depart from thy heart all the days of thy life: but teach them thy sons, and thy sons' sons* (Deuteronomy 4:9 KJV).

Again I found another scripture, Joel 1:3: *Tell ye your children of it, and let your children tell their children, and their children another generation.*

I found out things about my family just last year, things that I had gone through that could have been avoided. I wouldn't suggest that you tell your children such things when they are still children but when they have become mature young adults, it is appropriate. If you see them traveling down a road that you don't like, bring them aside and tell them about things you or your parents may have gone through so that they do not make the same mistakes. It is important to break those generational curses from your family line.

I could not believe I was back in England. It was a great feeling to see all my friends and family again but moving back under such a big black cloud was not the best feeling at all. It was awful. I put myself back in a position where I had to start again and rebuild my life. I had to prove to God, my parents, and to my family that I wanted to change and that I didn't like the person I had become.

I began to work for my uncle's church while trying to apply for a full-time job. I was able to get one steady job for six months but because of a lack of government funding, the program ended. I was an active member of my church. At this time, I met someone at another church. He was not my type—the total opposite. I did not find him attractive but I found myself giving this guy the time of day. (I'm rolling my eyes just thinking about all the time I wasted and I hate talking about it, but it has to be addressed.)

Now, this dude gave me attention—not the attention I needed or wanted but he gave it. I clearly was not healed from my first sexual experience at the age of sixteen and got myself involved with a man I should have stayed away from. We talked on the phone mostly and I told him I was a Christian and about the church I attended (big mistake). It took one time—yes, one time—meeting this person I had no business meeting alone and I ended up pregnant. I was under the impression we would be going to a movie and I was going to meet him at his apartment outside. He had no car, so how were we getting to the movies? But I chose— again, I *chose*—to meet this person. I remember lying down in his apartment thinking, *What the hell am I doing here?* (Yes, I said it because it was hell!) It smelled, he smelled. I mean, Lord have mercy. It was really such an awful experience.

After that whole experience, who shows up at my church the very next Sunday, and who does the usher sit me right next to as the church was packed and it was the only seat available? YES, you guessed it, the usher sat me right next to him. And this dude put his arm across the back of my seat as if we were together.

I could see my uncle looking at us as he preached and his face looked like he was thinking, *Now, who is this man sitting next to my niece with his hand on her chair?* I honestly don't know what my uncle was thinking but my mind was all over the place. I couldn't hear the Word, I could just feel the guy's hand on the back of my seat.

Straight after the service, I had a general conversation with him. I don't remember it word for word but I do remember I told him I had made a big mistake, I did not want a relationship with him and that what had happened between us would not happen again. Now, why did he continue to come to my church and then become a member, then date somebody else IN MY CHURCH? These were the consequences of my actions.

I began questioning God. "Why are you allowing this man to stay here? We can't both stay here. Lord, please, he has to go. Please, Lord, I can't take it."

I don't believe God allowed this to happen; I believe *I* allowed it to happen. I opened the door to this guy physically, which made him think he could walk into every other door that I had opened for him.

I realized I was pregnant at about three months and I booked an appointment for an abortion at the nearest clinic. In England, abortions are covered under the national health insurance, so you do not have to pay. Thinking back now, I still cannot believe that a twenty-year-old could go to an abortion clinic without a parent and ask for an abortion. But I was of age.

The day came when I was scheduled to go in for the abortion and I could not do it. I missed my appointment on purpose, then called the same clinic back a month later and tried to book another appointment. By that time, I was near the cut-off time where I could not have the procedure done so they advised that I travel to another clinic over an hour away. I decided to book the appointment, the date came, and I still could not do it. How could I get rid of my baby? I couldn't. I was scared and alone and I could not bring myself to tell anyone. Not even my best friend.

Have you ever seen an owner with a dog on a leash and it has a muzzle on its mouth? That's exactly how I pictured myself. I was the dog barking but there was a muzzle on my mouth and no one could hear me. My family are not bad people, they are good people. Had they known, they would have been disappointed, even angry, but I know now they would not have disowned me. It would have taken time but I know we would have gotten through it.

Being a pastor's kid and born into a family with such high standards haunted me. I had brought shame and disgrace upon God, myself, and my family. What I forgot was that the church I was attending had gone through this same situation before and they didn't treat the woman badly. I don't know why I couldn't see that they would still love me despite my flaws.

While pregnant, I continued on in ministry, even attending a biblically based program, which I think at that time saved my life. I thought the baby would just go away. A life was growing inside me, yet I did not want to live. I began cutting the tops of my arms, started to miss church, and at that time, I had moved out of my mother's home and moved into a family friend's home because we were constantly fighting. My mother did not know where I was or who I was staying with.

The lady I stayed with was an awesome person, a

beautiful woman of God who opened up her home to me not knowing what she was getting herself into. While living in her home, I delivered my baby boy myself on Saturday, June 7, 2008, at 4 a.m. People to this day ask me how I did it. I don't know. It was an out-of-body experience for me. The pain was bearable yet I didn't know what to expect afterward. When the afterbirth was coming out I thought it was another baby.

My baby was not breathing. Was I surprised? No, I wasn't. Was I scared? Yes, I was. I hadn't been to one doctor's appointment or check-up. I knew this was my fault and even then I still could not bring myself to call emergency services.

I sat with my baby for hours. When the lady I was staying with had left for the day, I left my baby boy wrapped up in a towel and slowly crawled down the stairs on my belly to the bathroom. I was renting an attic room so I was at the very top of the house. I was afraid to have a bath and thought that it would sting me but once I got in, it soothed me. I continued to lose blood and was exhausted. I managed to get out of the bath and crawled back upstairs, where I stayed with my baby all day. I wasn't in my right mind.

I caused my landlady tremendous heartache and pain as she was the one who later found my son. I had interrupted her life and her home. Your mess can certainly turn someone else's life upside down. Your actions do not just affect you, they affect everyone you are associated with, including family and friends. It hurts.

In the weeks to come, I was able to see her at a service. We both sat together while I poured my heart out and apologized. I continued to see her here and there throughout the years through travel. Sometimes I even felt that she was afraid of me.

Throughout my pregnancy, many people asked me if I was pregnant, from my father to my aunt. I lied. It was the easiest, most cowardly thing to do. My father said, "There is nothing you could ever do that could make us stop loving you," and even that did not help! I continued to stay STUCK! Stuck in the mud, stuck on stupid, just stuck! I was not ready for what was about to happen...

You know the saying "when life comes at you fast"? Well, it came at me at a hundred miles an hour!

7

Confess Your Sins One to Another

After the birth, I recuperated for a couple of days. Have you ever been in a daze? Your body is present but your mind is elsewhere? You're able to go to the bathroom, make dinner, catch a bus, and go to work but your spirit, your consciousness, is absent? I believe I was in a broken-down mental state. Mental health is real—it is not to be ignored or discounted. Your mental well-being is as important as your physical well-being. When you don't take care of your mental health, you will become empty and stone cold to the things that should really cause you to smile or laugh. It's a shame that in the black community, mental health is brushed under the carpet and isn't dealt with.

Well, I know you're wondering where the baby was. I

kept him in my room, wrapped in towels. Some ask, "How did you give birth by yourself? How did you go through all that pain? Why didn't you call for an ambulance? Why didn't you call for help?" I honestly do not have all the answers. I will never understand it myself but I do know I was beyond scared, in denial, and unwilling to face up to the demons that had haunted me for years. I put this little boy's life into my own hands and that I should never have done. I am not God. How dare I not call someone...anyone?

I gave birth to a baby boy who I later named Michael with the help of one of my aunts. His name means "who is like God." The Archangel Michael was the leader of soldiers in God's army in the heavens and I wanted to name my baby Michael because I believe he would have been a fighter, just like me.

I remember having a visit from my aunt, who was also my pastor, on the 9th of June. Unbeknownst to her, I had given birth on Saturday. That night she dreamt that I had given birth to a baby and had placed it in the bin. She woke up that Sunday morning troubled and was even more troubled after she received a phone call from me to say that I wouldn't be in church that Sunday. I didn't realize that she was in Scotland on a ministry trip. She was so concerned that she called my landlady and told her that she was coming to visit me on Monday after her return.

I was in my bedroom when my aunt arrived and she

came up to see me. As she entered the room, she saw a large red stain on the carpet, which she thought was strange. However, she had just one thing on her mind. She had purposed in her mind that she was going to look at my naked stomach to see once and for all whether I was pregnant or not. She came into the room, made a few inquiries about how I was feeling, then asked me to lift up my clothes so that she could see my stomach. When she saw my flat tummy, there was a look of confusion on her face and she didn't quite to know what to do.

My father had asked my aunt to accompany me to the doctor. I told her I had already gone and everything was fine. She wanted to know where I had been as I was absent from church, to see why I was so thin, and to just see what was going on with me in general. She saw the cuts on my arms. She tried to encourage me the best way she knew how, she prayed with me and let me cry on her shoulder, and I still couldn't find the courage to say I had just had a baby.

She talked to me for a short time, then we both went downstairs as my landlady wanted to speak to me with my aunt present. I guess this was due to my strange behavior over the past few months.

I look back even now and think about all the warnings and about all the help that was available to me at the time, yet I still could not bring myself to talk. Nothing, and I mean NOTHING, can ever be so bad that you cannot confess or confide. The Bible says, *If we confess our sins, He is faithful and righteous to forgive our sins and purify us from all unrighteousness* (the First Letter from John 1:9, TLV).

The key to unlocking the lies and deceit in this scripture for me was to confess. Had I confessed I was still having problems with promiscuity? Had I confessed I was pregnant? Had I confessed I was angry and bitter toward all three of my parents? If I had, maybe there would be a Michael today. Maybe I wouldn't have gone to see a man who clearly I had no business meeting. To actually sit and talk to someone who does not know you—someone who is a qualified counselor, someone who will make you see yourself before looking at or blaming anyone else—is the best thing a young teenager or a young adult can ever do. Before entering into relationships or marriage, please take the time to figure YOU out and dig into all those unresolved issues that might have you bound.

The Bible says, *But if you do not forgive others their sins, your Father will not forgive your sins* (Matthew 6:15). After you confess out of your mouth, you have to forgive. I've heard my parents say this many times. Having unforgiveness is like drinking a glass of poison and expecting your enemy to die. When we do not forgive, we are the ones who end up sick and cannot prosper. And we wonder why we are struggling.

While listening to my aunt speak in one of her messages, she said something that has stuck with me.

"While you're DYING in your expectations, people are really LIVING." Pastor Yvonne Brooks! We expect too much of man! We have so many excuses. My daddy left me when I was five...my mom was on drugs and left me on someone's doorstep...my uncle abused me when I was ten years old... Unfortunately, that's LIFE! Those are some horrific examples of how life can hit you and knock you off your feet. But how long are we going to hold people in bondage? Your mom, dad, and uncle have moved on, LIVING or DEAD, yet you are slowly but surely dying!

Life is a gift. This crisis in my life helped me to see that there is so much more to life than my pain. You are a king, you are a queen, you are born to reign and take dominion! Do not let your mistakes in life be your identity. A lot of people now see me as "the girl who got pregnant out of wedlock and hid her dead baby." I see myself as a strong woman, walking in God's divine purpose for my life, healed, delivered, and set free.

8

Back to the Beginning

I was going about my daily routine. I had locked my mother out of my life and thrown away the key. The sting of my parents' divorce lingered in my head, my emotions were deep-rooted, my bitterness had inflamed in me, and I was just exhausted, scared, and above all, LOST.

It was a summer night and I was walking home from church, talking on the phone as if it was a normal day. We come across people every day, be it on the bus, on the train, in church, or at work, and we never really know what is going on in someone's mind. A person can look as normal as can be while deep inside they are suffering silently.

Unbeknownst to me, earlier in the day, my landlady had found my baby hidden in the room upstairs. She immediately called my aunt, who was so shaken that she couldn't drive herself and had to get someone to drive her to the house. Upon her arrival, she demanded to see the baby but at the last moment could not face what she thought she would see.

They both came back downstairs and called my uncle, who was at a funeral in Nottingham. They decided that they would wait until he came and then they would call the police. In the meantime, my aunt called my father in the U.S. and explained what had taken place and the fact that they would have to call the police as there had been a birth and a death, and she did not know what the ramifications would be.

As soon as my uncle arrived, he instructed them to call the police. My landlady gave them the information over the phone, gave the address, and hung up. Immediately, the phone rang. It was the police asking if they had just made a report, while at the same time the front doorbell rang and the police had arrived.

They made my aunt, uncle, and my landlady wait in the living room while they secured my bedroom, which was now declared a crime scene. Within a few minutes, they had placed all three of them into a police van and whisked them off to the police station. It was between 9 and 10 o'clock at night. The police turned out the lights and waited in the house for me to arrive home.

A police officer met me at the door. He asked in a loud, blunt tone, "What is your name?"

I answered and he asked me if I knew why he was there.

I said, "Yes."

He then said to me, "I am arresting you on suspicion of murder."

He read me my rights, handcuffed me, and put me in the back of the police car, where a policewoman was waiting for me. The private investigator who handled my case told my father months after my ordeal that you are innocent until you are proven guilty in the U.S. but in the UK, it was different. In my case, I was presumed guilty. They had to prove I was innocent.

My life was no longer mine. It was in the hands of the judicial system. I had committed a crime and honestly, I was ready to serve my time. My body was exhausted, I had lost so much weight, and I continued to lose blood not knowing whether it was normal or not. I was relieved that the lie I had kept for months had been uncovered but I was also frightened, unsure of my future, and I dreaded the fact that I would now have to share this dreadful, ugly secret with my family. Crazy thoughts raced through my head as we drove down the quiet street and all I could see was the blue flashing lights from the police car.

I was afraid my mother would have some sort of anxiety attack, that my family in America would be distraught, and that my family in Stafford and Birmingham would feel the sting and pain of it all because it was so close to home. My thoughts were my reality. As the police took me away, I realized that the streets had been quiet when I was walking toward the door and now they were filled with flashing police lights and sirens. I was a criminal. They were going to take the child I had given birth to and I was never going to be with him again.

The policewoman asked me if I was still bleeding. I answered yes. As soon as I got to the police station, she gave me some thick pads, allowed me to use the toilet in front of her, and then booked me. She took my belt and put me on suicide watch.

While in the jail cell, I remembered the night before at church, when my uncle, who was my bishop at the time, was encouraging the congregation to come and confess at the altar. My uncle continued to encourage the congregation and the altar flooded with people. The musicians began to play a song titled "In Christ Alone!"

With tears running down my face, I cried like a baby on my cousin's shoulder and we both cried together. We held each other so tight. I didn't know whether she was going through anything at the time but I knew that I was going through hell on earth and I knew that God was giving me another chance to confess, to tell my cousin what was going on. God will give you chance after chance after chance! It's only for your good that He will expose your mess. But I could not bring myself to go down to the altar to confess.

I was arrested at about 10 p.m. and was then interviewed at about 12 a.m. by two psychologists and someone who represented me legally. The psychologist who sat opposite me, I know him to be the devil or a demon. I know the devil cannot be in more than one place at one time but I do know he sent one of his imps. His look was that of "you are going away for a very long time"—and he was glad about it! Some of his questions were: "Why didn't you throw the baby away? Why didn't you put him in the trash?"

Don't get me wrong, I know why I was asked those questions and I do know psychologists have a job to do, but I also know that the psychologist who sat next to him was an angel sent by God. He told me not to answer many of the questions and would word them differently. I know my family was rocked to the core and angry but I also know I had some praying parents, grandparents, aunts, and uncles who had me on their minds, interceding and petitioning to God for me.

At that time, my entire family was told that I had killed my baby. Imagine getting the news on the phone that your daughter, sister, granddaughter, niece, or cousin had concealed her pregnancy, had given birth by herself, and then killed her baby! Well, that's the news my family received. And for my dad to hear this news, and the rest of my family 3,000 miles away, was even more painful. Do you know that at this same time, three other stories were in the news on TV about women who had also concealed their pregnancies, given birth, and killed the babies? Luckily, my story was in a local newspaper in a tiny column on the front page, with no names mentioned. It was only God who made this happen.

My father shared this in our morning service. "Justice is when we get what we deserve; mercy is when we don't get what we deserve; and grace is when we get what we don't deserve." In America, the law states that you are innocent until proven guilty. In the United Kingdom, it states you are guilty until proven innocent.

Concealment of birth is a crime. The officer stated that I was looking at up to two years of jail time. I deserved to go to prison for two years. This was my crime.

During the time I was being evaluated, the lady I had been staying with was also going through interviews as well as my uncle and aunt. They were separated, their laptops and phones were taken, and they were accused, ridiculed, and interviewed like they were criminals. I felt so helpless and angry at myself that I had involved them in my shame and mess, along with the rest of my family. They now knew the deepest, darkest, ugliest secret I had hidden from them. And soon the church would know...and maybe even the world.

After being evaluated by the psychologists, I was returned to my cell. It was about 3 a.m. and the officer explained that in the morning, I would be taken to the hospital to be examined, then to court, and then later on in the day, I would be formally interviewed. It was about to be a long day.

9

What a Difference a Day Makes

At about 9 a.m. the police officers came to get me and we went straight to the hospital. When we got there, they took my handcuffs off my hands and feet. It then sank in that I was really a prisoner.

I was examined by a female doctor and was asked a few questions about the way I was feeling. One of the questions was whether I felt like I wanted to harm myself. After briefly explaining to the doctor what had happened, she looked at me with shock and said, "You are very strong to go through that whole labor by yourself. Do you know that women have died during labor because of hemorrhaging?" I nodded but it had not registered yet that I really could have died.

We then left the hospital and the two officers

transported me to court, where I would see the judge. I was placed in another holding cell and waited until it was my time. They came to get me about 30 minutes later and I was brought into the court and put in a box. I verified my name and address. No plea was requested at that time because the autopsy results had not come back from the coroner's office to rule out murder. I was so upset that the results had not come back yet. I wanted this whole ordeal to be over. I was tired, dirty, and emotionally drained. I knew what the results would say but waiting was my only option.

When your life is in someone else's hands you do not get to choose where you go, when you get up, or what to eat. Reality was sinking in. Even if the autopsy came back showing there was no foul play, I would still be going to prison for two years because of the concealment of birth charge.

The lawyer who represented me explained I would be spending another night in jail as a lot of details were still being investigated. The police had gone to my friends' houses and my mother's during their investigation, and had also gone to the father's home to take DNA samples. The father told everyone at that time I had been sleeping with numerous people and the baby could have been anybody's. The lies he told! But then again, we reap what we sow!

I was interviewed and taken back to my cell. While sitting there, I realized I had so much hatred for the baby's father. I knew the reason I didn't want to say anything about my pregnancy and felt shame and guilt over the 2.5 seconds that nearly ruined my life. I honestly felt like I had been with the devil! The father wasn't the quiet type, he was a very proud, loud and "in your face" type of dude. I actually felt quite embarrassed and after realizing he had four other children with different women, what a fool I was!

I had another 24 hours to think about what I had done, what I hadn't done, all the people I had hurt and lied to, and how my life would be during the next two years. Who was going to bury my baby? Would he have a proper burial? Would I be able to go? Would they put me in a psychiatric institute because what I had done was not normal? Would I ever recover? Would I ever really be able to live my life as a normal person? Would they think I needed to be medicated? What was going on in the outside world? How was my family? Could they ever forgive me? How could I have done this? What was wrong with me?

I could go on and on. My point is, I had time to think, time to reflect, time to worry, and time to stare. Yes, stare at the wall and look at the messages that previous prisoners had written.

I don't remember eating one thing while being in custody. I don't remember sleeping. I just remember being cold. I was sitting on a blue mattress, something like the play mat you would be given in physical education class, and there was a toilet. I think I mainly didn't eat because I did not want to use their toilet.

Thank God morning came. You wouldn't know it was morning as there were no windows. But one of the police officers came and opened my door, and took me to the interview room. I was still in the same dirty clothes, no shower or wash, but then who would really want to have a shower in jail? The officers asked me a couple of questions pertaining to the investigation. They told me the DNA results from Michael's father had come back positive. Well, duh! They then told me the postmortem exam revealed that Michael's lungs had not opened and there was no sign of strangulation or harm. It was a relief. Yet I still felt the sting of his death. He was still gone. I just cried and cried when they read the results.

After the interview, the officers turned the interview tape off, paused, then asked me where I wanted to live. I said, "Excuse me?"

The officer plainly said to me, "There must be someone up there looking out for you."

I will never forget those words. NEVER! I was convinced I was going to be incarcerated in a women's correctional facility or in a psych ward for two years. That's what they had told me in the beginning and I had trained my mind to think that way. They asked me whose home I wanted to go to.

"Your mom, your grandparents, your uncle and aunt, your friend...they have all opened their homes to you. So where do you want to go?"

I was thinking, *They actually want to see me?* Me, the person who lied and kept something so important from them? I couldn't believe it! I was too ashamed. I just wanted to run away.

Something came to mind while I was sitting there. When my father came out of his divorce with my mother, he said the one place where he felt like himself was Stafford, where he grew up, where his parents were and where the majority of his siblings were. And that's where I chose to go—to a place where there were still a lot of rules pertaining to your outward appearance...but did I really have time to think about that? No. All I wanted was love from my family although I didn't know what to expect. I just knew they wanted me and that was where I was going.

As soon as I got out, my auntie was waiting for me at the police station. I just cried. She hugged me and said I didn't have to talk. We drove the 30 minutes to Stafford.

The Bible says, *Trust in the Lord with all thine heart; and lean not unto thine own understanding. In all thy ways acknowledge him, and he shall direct thy paths* (Proverbs 3:5-6, KJV). One thing I did not do was trust that God could and would bring me out. I had come to the conclusion that this is what I deserved and many others also believed this. I'd had so many chances to change but chose not to. I was a law unto my own self! I had been found out, yet it was so easy for me to finally explain my story, to finally set myself free with the truth.

There is a saying that whatever is done in the dark will come to light. You cannot run from God; you cannot hide from God. When Eve hid herself away in the Garden of Eden after eating the fruit of the forbidden tree, shame and guilt instantly came upon her. She knew what she had done was wrong. No longer could she or Adam enjoy the benefits of this garden of life; they would suffer the consequences of their actions. As a Christian, I could not reap the benefits of a Christ-like life, living with all the unresolved issues I had stored in my heart over the years against the people I loved.

At twenty-one, I was still asking myself these questions: Why did my dad have to leave me? Did I do something wrong? Why was I born to parents that would divorce? Why did I see my dad show more love to his wife in America in their marriage than he did to my mother when they were married? My mother was miserable and angry but I'm the one that heard her hurt and pain. She was a Christian first, who happened to be the pastor's wife—the worship leader who sang songs of Zion, who was hurt and mistreated in the very church she had helped build by the very people in the church.

The single women loved my dad and were not discreet about it. It was sad and a shame to hear some of the things that happened, but like I said earlier, why did I, as a child, hear these things? It's not just parents who tell children things, it's also family members and church members. You think you can trust people with your business yet they run and tell the next person, even the children of the people you may be talking about. We need to begin to go up, meaning prayer and fasting or going to somebody that is not your friend, sister, cousin, or brother; someone who is of a higher position—a pastor, counselor, elder, minister...someone you can trust!

And that's why I say I do not want to be a preacher's wife or a pastor's wife. I have seen far too much of what my mother has gone through and I know it was God's strength that helped her.

10

Weeping May Endure For a Night But JOY Comes in the Morning

When we arrived in Stafford, my aunt drew me a bath and laid out some clothes for me to sleep in. My uncle (and then bishop) came to see me, hugged me, and asked me to tell him what had happened. I was not up to it, of course. I hadn't slept and I didn't want to sit down and face him—the man who had taken me under his wing; who had encouraged me in my gifts of administration, hospitality, and performing arts. But I owed him and my family more than an explanation. He just could not understand why I couldn't tell them and it pained me to see him so upset. All I kept thinking was, *What have I done?*

He explained to me that there had to be a church meeting for all members to be in attendance, and it would solely be about what had happened. I was an active member in the church and although I was quite disappointed that there had to be a meeting about me, it was the least of my worries. I hadn't spoken to my parents and family in America. *This* I dreaded.

I felt as though my head was in a bubble. Everything was happening outside of the bubble and everyone in the room was a blurred canvas. I wrote a brief statement for the church meeting that would be held the next day, hugged my uncle, then went upstairs to bed. I could hear the murmurs of my aunt and uncle talking downstairs and all I could do was cry.

While I lay in bed, my aunt brought me the phone. It was my daddy! As soon as I heard his voice it was so soothing to me, yet I felt his pain. I couldn't talk. I had no words. He encouraged me. He told me he loved me and there was nothing that I could ever do that could stop him from loving me. He ended by saying that he would be seeing me very soon. Even now, as I write this, tears come to my eyes.

Today, I have a very close relationship with my dad. I don't talk to him every day but he is my voice of reason and my hero, which makes me think, if I feel like this about my father, then what do I think of my Heavenly Father—the one who died for me, the one who dropped all my charges, the one who delivered me and set me free?

Oh, how His love amazes me! Delirious, a Christian band, sings a song called "Majesty" and there is a line in the song that says, "Your grace has found me just as I am, empty handed but alive in your hand." Wow! He loves me!

After I briefly spoke with my dad, he passed the phone to Pastor Connie. I listened. She asked me why I had done this. I could hear that she was angry with me. I couldn't speak. My dad was already coming to England as he had a speaking engagement so Pastor Connie asked me if I wanted her to come. I said yes but I was not sure of my answer. She then responded and said she thought it would be best that I spent my time with my dad. I agreed.

The aunt I stayed with bought me clothes. I remember being so skinny and not wanting to eat much. My aunt nursed me back to health, prayed with me, and was my shoulder to cry on. I think I cried every day for a very long time.

In the days leading up to Michael's funeral, I had a big argument with one of my aunties. Things were getting back to me, rumors about what people were calling me—a murderer! One family member even said that my father had created a monster. I think those two statements were the worst things that anybody has ever said to me in my life. It made me feel like people thought I was evil, that I was of the devil. It was an awful feeling.

The scripture says, *You belong to your father, the devil,*

and you want to carry out your father's desires. He was a murderer from the beginning, not holding to the truth, for there is no truth in him. When he lies, he speaks his native language, for he is a liar and the father of lies (KJV, John 8:44).

Whether I wanted to believe it or not, I realized that the devil had been my father for years! I was a liar. Did y'all just get a revelation? Because I just did. Lie upon lie to cover up the last lie I told. It's a vicious cycle.

Back to my aunt. We had an argument, which caused me to leave the home and run to my grandparents in tears. Now, my family in this small town all live within walking distance so I didn't run far. I banged on my grandparents' door, my grandma answered, I ran straight past my grandmother to my grandfather's room, laid myself down on his bed, and cried. This was the first time I had seen him since I had moved. It had been a couple of days since the long ride from the police station and I was scared. He was the patriarch of the family, the bishop who had planted churches across England, Jamaica, and America; who was strict and fully sold-out for Christ. The fact that I'd had sex outside of marriage, had lied and concealed my pregnancy...do you think I wanted to see this man, my grandfather? No way, no how!

Anyhow, at that point I needed to see him after days of avoiding him. While I lay sobbing on his bed, he asked me what had happened and why I was crying. That night, I poured my heart out to him. I told him everything from start to finish. He listened and listened and listened and then began to share with me something I will never forget. He chastised me for my sin and then blessed me. He prayed a father's blessing over my life! I cried and cried. What a release! I received healing through my tears.

Now, don't get me wrong—I was not totally healed but that was my first step toward my healing. I thank God for praying grandparents. I decided to stay there for the night.

I stayed in Stafford for about seven months. We had a funeral for Michael. Most of my family from England were present. The one family member who didn't come was one of my closest cousins. Everyone was angry and everyone had questions. It hurt me to see and to know I had hurt him so much that he couldn't come to the funeral. I was grateful that the rest of my family was able to be there but I know they were pained to see the little white-and-gold coffin I had picked out. It was just so small.

A few days before the funeral, I had gone to a baby store to pick out the burial clothes. I remember standing by the clothes and having an out-of-body experience. I couldn't believe I was picking out baby clothes for my dead baby. To think that I had put the fear of my family knowing I was pregnant before the life of my unborn son left me distraught. I also felt like certain people were only looking at the sin—"she lied"—instead of a life was lost due to the sin. This was just a horrific experience.

The funeral was private. I had asked for my mom and grandmother to ride with me in the funeral car and a sense of fear came over me as we approached the chapel. As I walked in, it was all a blur. My family was already in their seats. My eyes were wet with tears as I walked to my seat. The service was short and each one of my uncles read the scriptures I had requested of them. My pastor and uncle shared a word of prayer and final thoughts. It was a sad day—a very sad day I will not ever forget.

I don't think anyone knew what to say to me and the only thought I had was...*sorry*. The burial was like the actual death itself. My heart was torn apart. I also believe my family was ashamed. It was public news, a family filled with pastors and bishops, ministers and elders— how could this have transpired? It was a very difficult time for everyone.

Shortly after the funeral, my father arrived. Thank you, Jesus! My father retraced every one of my steps. He met with the church sister I had stayed with. He made sure the room I stayed in and had given birth in was redecorated and had new carpet, which was the least I could have done. We went back to the police station, where he spoke to the detectives who shared more light on the entire event. He spoke with my family. There were even people who wanted to see him, who were sending messages through one of my uncles that they had things to tell him that they thought he did not know about me. He declined. People will be just that, people. They all came out of the woodwork. But he made it clear to me that his sole purpose was *me*. He had come back for *me!* I had so much peace having him with me. I cried with him and I told him everything.

I did not go back to the congregation because of people's opinions and perceptions. I do believe my uncle and aunt had already made the decision for me not to return for a period of time. It's not something you can get over and I understood. Members of the church were angry and hurt and most of all, my family had to face it.

I was set up with a counselor recommended by the hospital I had been brought to the day after I was arrested. My father was able to meet her and we had a session together while he was visiting. I enrolled at the University of Wolverhampton and my father came with me to the open house. It was an awesome feeling to just have him there supporting me. I had dinner with both of my biological parents before my father left to return back to the U.S. This was not normal but it really helped me, seeing them together and with no arguments or fights. They were talking and getting along. I couldn't believe my eyes.

As a child, I hardly ever saw my parents together and happy. I don't remember seeing them kiss or hold hands. I'm sure they did but it was something I cannot remember. It felt like our home set-up was church first, then God, then your spouse and children when really it should have been God first, your spouse, family, and then the church. To see them having a normal conversation with each other was a gift to the eight-year-old child within me. I thank God today for mending our broken relationship.

Before my dad left he gave me a book titled *Daughters Gone Wild, Dads Gone Crazy*. We would read a couple of chapters together and talk about it afterward on the phone. It was our own project, something we could do together. I liked the idea. In fact, I *loved* the idea! In the book, the daughter was also a pastor's child who was brought up in a great home but then made a total turnaround for the worse and both the father and daughter had to figure out this beautiful thing called life. The father had come to the end of his rope and did everything he could to help his daughter get back on track.

My main focus now was to rebuild my relationships with those who wanted to rebuild an honest relationship with me. I remember receiving a Facebook message from the cousin who did not attend the funeral, about nine months after the ordeal. He actually apologized to me and let me know that he loved me. He said he would never understand what had happened but he was open to rebuilding a relationship with me. I was so happy to hear from him and at that point in my life, I actually believed that things would be all right. It really helped me. It felt like I was finally starting to get my family back.

11

It's a New Season, It's a New Day

I visited home in the USA in 2009. I had seen the parents only once since the birth and I was so happy to be getting away from home in England. I needed a break. I needed to see my family. I so badly wanted to just sit at my parents' feet.

I remember having a heart-to-heart with Pastor Connie and she told me straight, "You chose to lay down with that man. You may not have liked him, you may not have thought he was attractive, but it was something that you chose to do. You have to forgive him and you have to forgive yourself."

I realized then that I was still angry with Michael's father. I was thinking about my pregnancy, how I felt so alone with no one to talk to, no one to share the baby's first kick, no one to hold my hand with the first contraction, and no birth father at the funeral. I went through this all by myself. Yes, I know you are probably thinking that I chose to do the things I did. And yes, I did, but it still hurt to know that *I chose* to do it.

Pastor Connie helped me to look at myself first before I pointed the finger at anybody else. She explained to me that yes, bad decisions were made by family after everything was brought to light and it didn't take just one person to lay down and make a baby, but I had to own up to my actions. Sometimes you just gotta OWN IT.

I think because no one knew who the father was until maybe days, even weeks afterward, it felt like I was carrying this big load of crap on my shoulders. Have you ever watched the TV programs such as "Extreme Weight Loss Challenge" or "Celebrity Fit Club"? The trainer shows them how much they weigh in a different form, like some kind of meat or fat, and expects them to go on a hike carrying the exact amount that they're overweight. Well, this illustrates exactly how I was feeling. I felt like I was carrying the weight of the world on my shoulders!

In one of Pastor Connie's sermons, I heard her make such a great statement in her message regarding taking offense. She said, "I don't have enemies, I have a prayer list." WOW. I literally turned my hate for the man into prayer and prayed for him many times during my grieving process. It helped me get over him a lot quicker.

I do not pray for him now. He is not in my world and is a very distant memory—sometimes not even a memory at all. Do you know that I could not even remember my son's father's name a couple of years after what happened? And even now I have to think about it. God has a way of really erasing your hurt and those who hurt you without you even realizing it. I was talking to my friend about a few things and I could not remember the man's name! Because I was in a good place, I had forgiven him. I know it was God who made me forget and I had to chuckle at that.

What an awesome feeling it was to be back in the U.S. No one really knew my faults except for my family. I didn't get crazy looks, I didn't have to see the church folk in the mall or on public transportation. It was just a great feeling not to have to look over my shoulder constantly to avoid people who knew what had happened. It was the first time I had seen all of my siblings since the incident and it wasn't weird, like I thought it would be. They embraced me just like they normally did. Yes, they asked questions and I answered them as best I could. I apologized to every one of them and they responded with love. I wasn't surprised and I also felt like I was not alone. I do realize they were not present when everything came out, they were not in the heat of the turmoil that had broken so many relationships, but they still were my family.

While still in the U.S., I went to visit my Theo Therapist who I had been visiting since I was sixteen. I was now twenty-two. She is an older Caucasian lady and is just like a grandmother to me. I told her everything. I poured my heart out about all the events leading up to this day. She looked at me and said, "I am so proud of you." I looked at her, tears running down my face, with confusion. She explained to me the reason why.

I was going through counseling and was getting help. She said that's all it takes. She told me I needed to find out what my God-given purpose is and build my own personal relationship with God, and to see Him as my ultimate source.

At the beginning of 2014, my father started a series at church which is now our church vision, to be Saved, Healed, Delivered, Trained, Equipped, and Ministering. We, as the body of Christ, have so many people operating in the ministry who are *saved* but not *healed*, *saved* but not *delivered*, or *saved* but not *trained*. We, as a church, had to go back to basics.

The first message was called "Am I Saved?" We were to ask ourselves that question. From that message, I realized that I hadn't fully given my life to the Father until I was twenty-one years of age. I may have gotten baptized at the age of ten but I know I did not get saved until the age of twenty-one. I was still thinking I could get away with a lot of things until I got caught. A lot of times, it isn't really until we are caught in a lie or simply just caught in our sin before we are made to face the ugliness of ourselves. Yes, I have made other mistakes since then but that's why Paul tells us in Corinthians

15:31 (KJV) that we have to die daily, repent of our sins.

Ephesians 4:26 (KJV) says, *Be ye angry and sin not; let not the sun go down on your wrath.*

It's OK to be angry at people or yourself but don't let it cause you to sin against God. Let go quickly, be quick to apologize even when you are not at fault, and be the peacemaker in every situation. Let God be pleased with your worship. I find that now, because I am part of the worship team at my church, I cannot and will not go up there without making sure my hands are clean. Repentance is the way forward and never do I want to go before God knowing I have sinned. It is too high a cost to pay.

Some of my family members back in the UK were still not speaking to me and that was one of the hardest things to deal with. Your family sees you at your lowest points as well as the greatest moments in your life. When sin is something that you choose, God will take His hands off of you. And this is exactly what some of my family chose to do. I can understand it but it still hurts. You never want God to take His hands off of your life. It will be harder to live and harder to survive. I want Him in every area of my life. I want to see His love, His greatness, and His awesome power in my life and for this, I have to be the best Sophia I can be! God is higher than my family, and as long as I am forgiven by Him, I have to choose to move on.

My uncle shared with me a statement I will never

forget. He said that my greatest revenge would be to become a massive success and to bring my enemies to shame. It has stuck with me ever since and I am determined to be just that, a MASSIVE SUCCESS.

My parents in the U.S. and my mom in the UK were there with me every step of the way while I was staying with my grandparents on my way to recovery. Whether it was on the phone, through email, or prayer, I was so grateful for their support.

I was scheduled to meet with an LPC (Licensed Professional Counselor) every week for about two to three months. It was one of the best decisions I made. We would meet at my grandparents' and talk for about an hour and a half about life. I was grateful for this time! The counselor made me see *me*. I found through our sessions that I complained too much. I remember listening to a teaching from John Bevere regarding the Bait of Satan. He said, "God hates complaining and you should treat it as poison. It's like I'm telling God, 'You have made a mistake, Lord, and I can do it better.'"

There has to come a time where we stop blaming the world, stop complaining, and just say Lord, I repent! I'm sorry, it was me. I had to come to a point in my life where I was quick to apologize and quick to embrace.

I was grateful to my grandparents. They took care of me for nearly a whole year before I went back to live with my mother. They are great people, loyal people, and family is very important to them. I love them. And if they are reading this, I just want to say thank you. I love you.

I know they loved having me around but I couldn't help but feel like a burden. I had started university in my hometown and the commute from Stafford was about twenty minutes on the train. So, I decided to move back with my mother. It was a different me and it was a different mother. Sometimes I would catch her looking at me with such sorrow. She was sad for me. I understood her sadness but I didn't want her to concentrate on what had happened. I wanted her to also heal and move forward.

We took care of each other this time. I was sensitive to her feelings and she was sensitive to mine. It was perfect. I knew she had questions that she needed answers to and so did I, but I decided those questions I had would be written in a letter and then destroyed. In Theo Therapy, the Christian-based counseling I mentioned earlier in the book, I learned how to write letters to God, to my parents, and others. My letter would start off with *Dear whoever, I am angry because...* or *This hurt me because... I choose to forgive you because...*

Some things are better left unsaid. Once the letter was written, I would read it, rip it up, exhale, and breathe. LET IT GO. As humans, we hold on to things, people, and situations we cannot change and it can literally start to make you sick. We need to learn to let it go. The person you are mad at has moved on. It might seem like God is blessing them—a new car, new house, engagement, new job, marriage, anything—and you're still angry. Concentrate on you and you alone. God has something great in store for you. He is just waiting for you to drop off all that baggage you are holding on to so you can walk into your purpose and destiny. For all the hell you have been through, there is a way out, there is a way forward.

Pastor Connie tells us every year to make sure we make new friends. You never know who holds your key to the next door that God has before you. If trust is a big issue for you, get over it. People are going to hurt us. It's how we react that will change the whole nature of the game. My parents teach on this all the time—when a person has hurt you, you do have to forgive them but one thing you do not have to do is reconcile and bring that person back into your circle. My granddad says this all the time: "Sometimes you just have to love people from afar."

If God is for you, who can be against you? Isaiah 54:17 reads, *No weapon that is formed against thee shall prosper; and every tongue that shall rise against thee in judgment thou shalt condemn. This is the heritage of the servants of the Lord, and their righteousness is of me, saith the Lord* (KJV). Weapons will be formed but they will not prosper, they will not succeed. Pray for those who despitefully use you, that's what the Good Book says.

About a year later, I received an unexpected call from my uncle, the bishop of the church I had previously attended. He was inviting me back to the church to address the congregation. I was so nervous but I knew this was something I had to do. It was there where so many people loved me and wanted to see the best for me, and only a few saw the worst. So I wrote a speech because I knew I wouldn't be able to speak without losing my thought process or crying the whole way through. I called the parents in the U.S. and asked them to help me pen out my speech.

After I felt it was ready and let my uncle know I was ready, I made my way to the church and my cousin met me at the door. It was so good to see her. It was a new church facility. So much had changed within a year of me leaving. She escorted me to my uncle's office while Bible class was going on. It was so good to see him. He had been like a father to me in so many ways when my father left to go to the U.S.

We spoke briefly. I read him my speech and asked if it was OK. He said it was good. Just before the service ended, he walked me out to the sanctuary. I saw my auntie, who gave me a great big squeeze. Then he asked me to sit in the front row. I sat their anxiously, waiting for my turn to speak. Right then and there I asked God to help control my tears and help me get through it.

Uncle introduced me and I went up and took the microphone. With tears running down my face, I apologized and let the congregation know that I was on my way to recovery. My uncle then stood by me and told me in front of everybody, if anybody in the church had anything to say to me or ask me they would get their answers from him. This gave me great comfort. I was so grateful to God for allowing my uncle to stand in the gap for me at that time, although it had been so long. He told the congregation that he and my aunt stood with me and would be there for me. The sense of relief that flooded my soul was just such an amazing feeling.

What the enemy made for evil, God turned around for my good. I was in awe of God's presence. I felt His presence with me and I was grateful. The congregation was invited to welcome me back to the church and I had to stand at the front while the members came and addressed me. Some came with hugs, words from the Lord, and some not so good comments but I received the good and let go of the negative. It was good to be home.

I had been visiting a church in the town where I lived with my mother when I moved back. It's there where I met some of my greatest friends. Timothy, Sabrina, Trina, and Shereen, thank you for being my friends, for not judging me, and for being great listeners. I love you. The church, funny enough, has the same name as my parents' church in the U.S.

After reconciling back to my uncle's church I began to attend services again. It wasn't easy but with the support of all of my family, I was able to attend with my head held high. Never proud but always humble.

It was really hard for me after university to find a

job. I had a government-funded job that was great pay but due to a lack of funding, my contract ended after six months. I became very frustrated. My uncle and aunt employed me at the church for a period of time, which was very helpful. After looking and looking for more permanent work and not finding anything, I had to sit down and re-evaluate my circumstances.

I looked at the pros and cons of living in the UK and the USA. I had to go back to my drawing board and speak to my parents in the U.S. I wanted to stay in the UK to prove to all of my naysayers that I had made it. What happened in my life didn't stop me from becoming the better person I knew I could be. But we really cannot live our lives for anybody else but ourselves. I had to make the right decision for me and that meant asking my parents about moving back to the U.S.

I did not know what they would say. I had caused them a lot of heartache and pain, just as I had with my family here, but the only thing I could do was ask. There were no open doors for me in the UK but many doors that would be open to me in the U.S., especially for jobs.

Once I made the decision, I emailed my parents and asked if I could come home. I explained my situation. It was 2011, three years after what had happened, and I needed to make some major changes. Both parents responded and said yes.

Now, the reason they said yes was because they knew I had changed. I wasn't the wounded girl who felt hurt, abandoned, and rejected. I was a young lady now who stood in the confidence of knowing that she was forgiven, loved, and appreciated. I was still receiving help from my therapist and I was on the right track. I sent my parents the money I had saved up for my ticket and I was to move back in November. My mom in the UK was sad but she knew it was the right decision for me. I let my whole family know my plans and they too were sad that I was leaving.

12

Home from Home

I honestly felt like I had made the right decision. A month before I returned to the U.S., Pastor Connie asked me to send my resume and my one-year plan. I had originally set a goal of living by myself by 2013. It was now 2011. Pastor Connie said all the things I had listed could be done in one year. In my head, I was thinking, *Yeah, right...not possible.*

This was my list for 2011-2012: get a full-time job, permit, driving lessons, license, buy a car, acquire insurance, and move out. I asked myself, could I really do this in a year? Pastor Connie said, "Yes, you can." I applied to all the retail stores I could think of as Christmas was just around the corner. After two weeks of being home in the USA, I started a temporary job at a retail store two minutes from home and my parents made sure I had a second income working part-time as the administrative assistant at the church. I was so grateful to have two incomes within the space of two weeks of coming home. I was so very grateful that God continued to be faithful.

My first job interview was at a health insurance company the beginning of December. I got the call the beginning of January 2012 that they wanted me to start in two weeks. God was working it out for my good. I was simply amazed by His goodness toward me. He didn't have to do it, I was so unworthy of it, but He thought of me as worthy. When God says move, you move! No questions asked. Just like Nike's slogan, "Just do it!"

Pastor Connie sent my resume to many different companies before I arrived and prayed that my transition back home would be smooth—and it went just that way. I got my learner's permit in February and passed my driver's test for my license the beginning of May. I then bought my first car in June and moved into a two-bedroom apartment with my oldest sister in August. Within nine months of me moving back home, my life had accelerated. The term for that year was the "Year of Acceleration." What it takes most people years to accomplish only took me nine months.

Although looking back I do feel that I needed more time to settle in, I understood how important it was for me to stand on my own two feet. Do you see how fast God can do a work in your life when you are in the will of

God? I was just in awe of God's favor in my life. And I know it had a lot to do with the favor of God on my parents' life. It was up to me to make the decision to ask my parents to move back. I had to make a choice. staying in England was not helping me move forward in life. Although I was getting the counseling I needed and was surrounded by family and great new friends, part of my life felt like it was standing still.

Family life in the U.S. still had its challenges. Trust issues were a big problem with the parents and some of my siblings. I found myself still apologizing for things that had happened in my past which I knew I had already apologized for, and my behavior in the past kept them thinking I wasn't being truthful.

My dad shared with me something that helped me with my process of letting myself off the hook. He said that people, even family, ten years from now will still see the person I once was. They will not be able to get over what happened. He told me to never answer the call to my past. I do not owe one single person an explanation. My sin was thrown into the sea of forgetfulness. I knew my family wanted the best for me, so thank God we were able to get through it.

I am still here and I am still learning. Life is still throwing its challenges at me but I remember that I am blessed to still be walking this earth and breathing the breath of life. I miss my mom a great deal. Although we had many challenges while I was growing up, she is still always there for me. I had to stop thinking, *If I leave, Mom is going to be by herself.* I had to start living my life and making something of myself. It was time to put Sophia first and stop having this mindset of having to please the people around me. I had to discover my purpose in life and figure out why I am here on this earth and who I am supposed to help and empower.

What positive things can come out of a broken home, a concealed pregnancy, and sexual immorality? I decided to tell you my story. I want my life to be a positive testimony to men and women that you don't have to continue the life that you are living and you don't have to suffer in silence. Speak up! You have a voice. And if you are recovering from a stillbirth, the death of a child, or separation from a parent or loved one, there are support groups and organizations that can help you through it. You are not alone.

I just want to encourage everybody out there to fight for your dreams. Having a baby out of wedlock is not the end of the world. GET BACK UP, fight for your life, and fight for your dreams! Stop hanging around the wrong crowd. Cut off the people that are only taking from your life and not adding. Go back to school if you need to, finish high school, finish university—whatever you have left undone, finish it.

Hebrews 10:25 (KJV) says: *Not forsaking the assembling of ourselves together, as the manner of some is; but exhorting one another: and so much more, as ye see the day approaching.*

Find yourself a church home if you don't already have one. No church is perfect but try to find a healthy church that is striving to be holy and acceptable. My father always says a sheep without a shepherd is lost.

Today I am truly living my life like it is golden. I'm appreciative of the small things as well as the bigger things that are happening for me. I am free from bondage and I am still seeking inner healing. I choose to live a life of no regrets, learning from my mistakes and pursuing God like never before. I want to make it to Heaven, I don't want to go to Hell. I am determined to see Jesus, the Savior of my soul, at those pearly white gates and I am determined to hear Him say, "Well done, thy good and faithful servant."

My goal in life is to help other pastors' children who have suffered in silence, to share my story on a deeper level, and encourage them so they know that they too have hope.

There is not a day that goes by that I don't think about my baby boy. I see his face and there are still times when I have moments of tears and sadness. I remember when I started writing this book, all the emotions came back and all the pain. It was a rehearsal night and thankfully Pastor Connie was at church. I just cried and cried. He is always going to be a part of me. Every year on his birthday, I buy a pack of baby-blue balloons and go to the local park. I say a prayer and release them into the sky. His grave is back in the UK and my mother and a few family members take care of it. I know he is not there but it would be nice to go there on a challenging day to sit and spend time.

In 2017, my family and I were able to finally buy his headstone after nearly ten years. The overwhelming emotion of visiting the grave and seeing the stone with my mother and father, sister, nephew, and cousins, who came to support me, was priceless. I felt a huge part of my heart begin to heal. I guess it was closure for me. It is hard but I am comforted by the fact that I will see Michael again. His death cannot be in vain. He became a sacrifice for me so I am determined to live my life with purpose and be a blessing to others.

And when God finally blesses me with my future husband, I don't plan on being broken. I don't plan on giving fifty percent to my marriage. I plan on being whole. I want to be able to give him my all. He deserves to have a woman healed and delivered instead of broken and wounded. Marriage is a sacred union and is one of the desires of my heart. I plan on enjoying every minute of it. Divorce is not an option.

My future with Jesus looks so bright!

For Parents

■ ■ ■

A Mother's Love

When a family breaks down (divorce) and the children involved are of a certain age, they must be protected at all costs from the fallout. Explain to them that it's not their fault, that Mummy and Daddy love them very much. Saddened as they will be, children are resilient. Problems arise when the children are manipulated or torn between both parents because of negative and conflicting information they receive, verbal and nonverbal, resulting in devastating consequences for years to come. So, for the purpose of damage limitation, we must protect them. We marry for life but when divorce happens, it's never black or white. There are gray areas too.

And so, I exhort grandmothers, grandfathers, aunties, uncles, cousins, and church families, if the above is happening in your family, it is imperative that you let the children know that they are loved by both parents. Let them know that their Mummy and Daddy are going through a difficult time. If you feel embittered toward one party or the other, under no circumstances do you convey that to the children. Remember, actions speak louder than words. "The Letter Kills but the Spirit Gives Life." If children want to talk, talk to them together. If they are led to believe that one parent is at fault, it will be a travesty. The time will come when, as adults, they will be mature enough to understand for themselves and see the bigger picture.

Thank God that Sophia survived to tell her story about how she overcame.

Yours Sincerely,

A Proud Mother

A Father's Love

Parenting in the 21st century has never been more difficult. If there ever was a time when we needed to adhere to the biblical world view on the family, it is now.

Sophia's story, though punctured with tragedy and disappointment, is a glowing testimony of God's grace and providence during the most difficult and dark times in her life. Even though sometimes I failed Sophia, our Lord never failed to father her.

When my daughter was feeling abandoned and alone, her Heavenly Father was there. When the devil wanted to take her life, her Heavenly Father said no. When he wanted to derail her destiny and destroy her future, her Heavenly Father said no. When the devil demanded that her uncle, aunt, and the church they pastored be mired in shame and disgrace, our Heavenly Father said no. And when the devil wanted to make my daughter's pain a national headline and tabloid news, our Heavenly Father said no.

During Sophia's season of rebellion, I reached the point of no return and had made up my mind to walk away and close my heart, but OUR Heavenly Father said, "No. I didn't walk away from you or close my heart to you."

So, I encourage every parent whose son or daughter

has disrespected and disregarded them to NEVER close your heart to your child because when your prodigal child returns, you will be able and willing to forgive and reconcile.

— Pastor Neville Brooks

A Stepmother's Love

Sophia, congratulations on completing your book! I know it will touch the lives of many, especially young adults who have been tested and tried. After reading your book, they will know they can recover just like you did. You made it through such an ordeal and survived to tell the story. I am glad that you are part of my life and know that I'll always be here to pray for you, stand with you, and to be an encouragement to you. Now, go forward and be the best psalmist, speaker, and writer!

— Apostle Connie Brooks

About the Author

Sophia Jennifer Brooks was born in the United Kingdom and was a source of pride for her parents, Neville Brooks and Beverly Clark.

Since moving to the United States, Sophia has been a member of Jubilee International Ministries in Pittsburgh, PA, where her parents, Neville and Connie Brooks, are the Overseer and Senior Pastor and Apostle. She is one of the praise-and-worship leaders, has been instrumental in many of the events planned at Jubilee, and was an integral part of the Sick and Shut-in Department.

She is on the board of directors of "A Gospel Musical: From Chains to Gains" and performs with the ensemble. This musical will take you on a historical journey of Black history. This year, 2018, is the third year of this production being performed. The fourth performance was at the Three Rivers Arts Festival in downtown Pittsburgh.

Sophia believes that NOW is the time for her story to be told so that other people can be encouraged and restored back to Christ. It doesn't matter what you have done, as long as you confess with your mouth and believe in your heart that God is faithful to turn your situation around. He changes your mess into your message; your test(s) into your testimony.

In the words of the songwriter, "This is my story, this is my song, praising my Savior all the day long" for what He's done for me.

Be blessed!

Contact the Author

Facebook - Sophia Brooks

Instagram- Mz Brux

Twitter- Mz Brux

Support Groups

IMMEDIATE DANGER: 911

NATIONAL SUICIDE PREVENTION LIFELINE
1-800-273-8255

CDC NATIONAL SEXUALLY TRANSMITTED DISEASES
1-800-227-8922

GRIEF RECOVERY LINE
1-800-445-4808

NATIONAL MENTAL HEALTH ASSOCIATION
1-800-969-6642

ABORTION HOTLINE
1-800-772-9100

COMPASSIONATE FRIENDS
(for parents enduring the loss of a child)
1-630-990-0010

CENTER FOR ADOPTION SUPPORT
www.adoptionsupport.org

MOTHERS IN SYMPATHY & SUPPORT
www.missfoundation.org

PITTSBURGH INTEGRATIVE MENTAL HEALTH
www.pimhservices.com

*Please note that telephone numbers & contact
information might change.*

31665603R00069

Printed in Poland
by Amazon Fulfillment
Poland Sp. z o.o., Wrocław